Animals and Us

FUSION

Service Animals

By E. C. Andrews

BEARPORT PUBLISHING

Minneapolis, Minnesota

Credits
All images are courtesy of Shutterstock.com, unless otherwise specified. With thanks toAlamy, Getty Images, Thinkstock Photo, and iStockphoto. Recurring – Viktoriia Ablohina. Cover – hchavda. TOC – David P Baileys. 2–3 – SasaStock. 4–5 – 24K-Production, Africa Studio. 6–7 – JoAnn Gilpin, Jami430, CC BY-SA 4.0 <https://creativecommons.org/licenses/by-sa/4.0>, via Wikimedia Commons. 8–9 – Eric Isselee, Roman Chazov, fotografixx. 10–11 – Westend61, Belish. 12–13 – Steve Shoup, FG Trade Latin. 14–15 – georgeclerk, Frazao Studio Latino. 16–17 – Piotr Piatrouski, ESB Professional, Tribune Content Agency LLC. 18–19 – Yuliya Evstratenko, Tatjana Baibakova. 20–21 –Michael Andersen, CC BY-SA 2.0 <https://creativecommons.org/licenses/by-sa/2.0>, via Wikimedia Commons, Frederic Dieupart. 22–23 – Mark Umbrella, SeventyFour.

Bearport Publishing Company Product Development Team
Publisher: Jen Jenson; Director of Product Development: Spencer Brinker; Managing Editor: Allison Juda; Editor: Cole Nelson; Associate Editor: Naomi Reich; Associate Editor: Tiana Tran; Art Director: Colin O'Dea; Designer: Kim Jones; Designer: Kayla Eggert; Product Development Specialist: Owen Hamlin

Library of Congress Cataloging-in-Publication Data is available at www.loc.gov or upon request from the publisher.

ISBN: 979-8-89232-731-2 (hardcover)
ISBN: 979-8-89232-781-7 (paperback)
ISBN: 979-8-89232-818-0 (ebook)

For more information, write to Bearport Publishing, 5357 Penn Avenue South, Minneapolis, MN 55419.

Contents

WHAT ARE Service Animals?

Working animals help us in a lot of ways. Some of them help people with **disabilities**. These clever, furry workers are called service animals.

There are many different kinds of disabilities. Not all can be seen.

Service animals are allowed in many places that other animals are not. When you see a working service animal, give them space to do their job.

Some service animals wear vests or harnesses that let people know they are working.

A Special KIND OF Animal

Service animal training can take one to two years.

The first step to becoming a service animal is training. The animal works with a **handler** who teaches them what their owner needs and how to help. The animal is trained to keep an eye on their owner and be ready to act quickly.

All this training is a lot of work. Not all animals are right for working jobs. Only the best of the best become service animals.

Animals that do not finish training are adopted as pets.

GUIDE Dogs

Sometimes, people who are **blind** or cannot see clearly get furry helpers to move around safely. Guide dogs can lead them through crowded spaces. These dogs keep their owners from bumping into or tripping over things in the way.

Guide dogs wear a harness with a handle that their owners can hold.

Guide dogs can follow commands to help their owners find things, such as a door or a chair. These dogs are also trained to help their owners cross the road and get up and down stairs safely.

People who are blind may also use canes to help them move through the world.

Guide dogs start their basic training when they are puppies. They learn commands such as sit, stay, and walk forward. This will help them later during guide dog training.

Guide dogs practice moving through different kinds of spaces.

Many of these dogs start their guide training when they are around 14 to 18 months old. They learn to walk just in front of their handler. This lets the animal lead the way along a path.

HEARING Dogs

A hearing dog acts as their owner's ears.

Hearing dogs help people who are **deaf** or cannot hear very well. These furry workers are trained to warn their owners about different sounds.

When the working dog hears a sound, it will **alert** its owner. It may nudge or paw to get their attention. Then, the hearing dog leads them to where the sound is coming from.

Hearing dog training starts with learning how to work even when there are loud things around. The dogs practice taking walks in busy places.

It can take hundreds of hours to train a hearing dog.

These dogs are also taught to **react** to some sounds very quickly. If a hearing dog hears sounds from smoke alarms, phones, doorbells, or alarm clocks, they let their owner know right away.

SEIZURE Response Dogs

Seizure (SEE-zhur) response dogs are trained to help their owners before, during, or after a seizure. A person who has a seizure may fall and hurt themselves. Being ready and getting help quickly is important.

Some seizures can cause a person to lose control of their body.

These response dogs alert people around them by barking or pressing a button to set off an alarm. Seizure dogs must learn ways to keep their owners from being hurt during seizures.

Sometimes, a seizure alert dog will lay on top of its owner to keep them safe.

ALLERGY Detection Dogs

Some dogs can sniff out things people have **allergies** to. Allergy **detection** dogs use their noses to check food and drinks. Then, they let their owner know if those items are safe to eat or drink.

Common allergies include milk and peanuts.

Allergy detection dogs can make life easier for people with serious allergies. These dogs help their owners feel safe when eating, drinking, or going outside.

GUIDE Horses

While most service animals are dogs, they are not the only animals helping humans. Ponies and other small horses can also work! These hoofed animals help people who are blind or cannot see very well find their way around safely.

Horses can live for up to 30 years!

Guide horses have great eyesight. They can see well at night, too. Some horse bodies are strong and tall enough for their owners to lean into as the animals lead them around.

Service Animals AND US

There are many kinds of service animals that help those who need it in different ways. They play an important role in keeping people safe, solving problems, and making their owners' lives easier.

Always treat working animals with love and respect. Taking good care of these animals helps them stay strong, happy, and healthy while they work.

Service animals help people feel safe wherever they go.

Glossary

adopted taken in as part of a family

alert to let someone know

allergies medical conditions that cause people to become sick after eating, touching, or breathing something

blind unable to see

deaf not able to hear

detection finding or discovering something

disabilities conditions that make it hard for people to go about everyday living

handler a person who trains and works with animals

react to change in response to something

seizure a sudden attack that can cause a person to shake and sometimes lose consciousness

Index